THE HISPANIC INFLUENCE IN THE UNITED STATES

LATINOS
IN AMERICAN HISTORY

JUAN PONCE
DE LEON

BY JIM WHITING

Mitchell Lane
PUBLISHERS

P.O. Box 619
Bear, Delaware 19701

THE HISPANIC INFLUENCE IN THE UNITED STATES

LATINOS
IN AMERICAN HISTORY

OTHER TITLES IN THE SERIES

Alvar Nuñez Cabeza de Vaca

Hernando de Soto

Juan Ponce de Leon

Pedro Menendez de Aviles

Gaspar de Portola

Mariano Guadalupe Vallejo

Francisco Vasquez de Coronado

Lorenzo de Zavala

Dolores Huerta

Jovita Idar

Octaviano Larrazola

Fray Juan Crespi

Americo Paredes

Juan Bautista de Anza

Diego Rivera

Juan Rodriguez Cabrillo

Miguel Jose Serra

Bernardo de Galvez

Visit us on the web: www.mitchelllane.com
Comments? email us: mitchelllane@mitchelllane.com

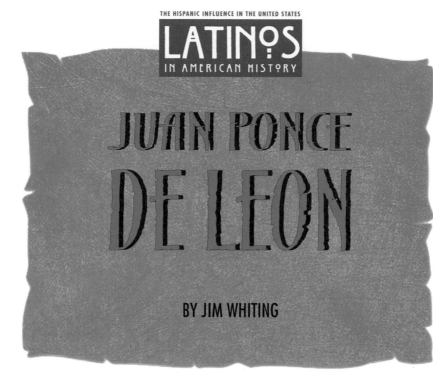

THE HISPANIC INFLUENCE IN THE UNITED STATES

LATINOS
IN AMERICAN HISTORY

JUAN PONCE
DE LEON

BY JIM WHITING

Mitchell Lane
PUBLISHERS

Printing 1   2   3   4   5   6   7   8   9

Library of Congress Cataloging-in-Publication Data

Whiting, Jim, 1943-
  Juan Ponce de León / Jim Whiting
    p. cm. — (Latinos in American history)
    Summary: Describes the life of the Spanish explorer who first came to the New World with Columbus, went on to become governor of Puerto Rico, and later came to Florida looking for the Fountain of Youth.
    Includes bibliographical references and index.
    ISBN 1-58415-149-8
    1. Ponce de Leân, Juan, 1460?-1521—Juvenile literature. 2. Explorers—America—Biography—Juvenile literature. 3. Explorers—Spain—Biography—Juvenile literature. 4. America—Discovery and exploration—Spanish—Juvenile literature. [1. Ponce de Leân, Juan, 1460?-1521. 2. Explorers. 3. America—Discovery and exploration—Spanish.] I. Title. II. Series.
    E125.P7 W48 2003
    972.9'02'092—dc21
    [B]   2002022143

ABOUT THE AUTHOR: Jim Whiting has been a journalist, writer, editor, and photographer for more than 20 years. In addition to a lengthy stint as publisher of *Northwest Runner* magazine, Mr. Whiting has contributed to the *Seattle Times*, *Conde Nast Traveler*, *Newsday*, and *Saturday Evening Post*. He has edited more than 20 titles in the Mitchell Lane Real-Life Reader Biography series and Unlocking the Secrets of Science. He lives in Washington state with his wife and two teenage sons.

PHOTO CREDITS: Cover: Hulton/Archive; p. 6 Archivo Iconografico, S.A./Corbis; p. 12 North Wind Picture Archives; p. 16 Jeremy Horner/Corbis; p. 18 Hulton/Archive; p. 22 North Wind Picture Archives; p. 28 Cummer Museum of Art & Gardens/SuperStock; p. 34 Hulton/Archive; p. 38 North Wind Picture Archives; p. 39 North Wind Picture Archives; p. 40 Jeremy Horner/Corbis; p. 42 Bettmann/Corbis; p. 44 Hulton/Archive; p. 46 Wolfgang Kaehler/Corbis; p. 47 Tony Arruza/Corbis; p. 48 Bettmann/Corbis.

PUBLISHER'S NOTE: This story is based on the author's extensive research, which he believes to be accurate. Some parts of the text might have been created by the author based on his research to illustrate what might have happened years ago, and is solely an aid to readability for young adults.

The spelling of the names in this book follow the generally accepted usage of modern day. The spelling of Spanish names in English has evolved over time with no consistency. Many names have been anglicized and no longer use the accent marks or any Spanish grammar. Others have retained the Spanish grammar. Hence, we refer to Hernando de Soto as "de Soto," but Francisco Vásquez de Coronado as "Coronado." There are other variances as well. Some sources might spell Vásquez as Vazquez. For the most part, we have adapted the more widely recognized spellings.

CONTENTS

This painting depicts Christopher Columbus, who was the first European explorer to discover America. He had trouble recruiting enough sailors to man the three ships he used for his first expedition in 1492. When word spread of the riches that he had discovered, he didn't have any problems for his next voyage. It began late in 1493 and included 17 ships and 1,200 men. One of those men was Juan Ponce de León.

TIERRA! TIERRA!

Early on the morning of November 3, 1493, lookouts perched in tiny crow's-nests high above the decks of a fleet of 17 sailing ships began screaming, *"Tierra! Tierra!"* *Tierra* means "land" in Spanish.

The thrilling news spread quickly through the ships Hundreds of men, still rubbing sleep from their eyes, rushed on deck and began talking excitedly among themselves. Their long days at sea were almost over.

Their voyage had begun on the morning of September 25 in the port city of Cádiz, Spain. About six months before that, Christopher Columbus had returned to Spain with the exciting news that he had discovered a fabulous new world.

He had departed from Palos, about 50 miles up the Spanish coast from Cádiz, for his voyage of exploration on August 3, 1492, but then he only had three ships—the *Niña*, the *Pinta* and the *Santa Maria*. Because he was venturing into unknown, uncharted waters, he had had problems recruiting enough men to provide adequate crews for his three ships.

Not this time. As soon as he set foot on Spanish soil, reports of what he had discovered—some true, some false, but all wonderful—began spreading like wildfire throughout the countryside. Columbus quickly announced that he would make a return trip. Unlike the first voyage, this time people would stay to establish colonies. Excited by reports that gold and other riches awaited them in abundance, thousands of men wanted to sail with Columbus.

From that huge group, Columbus picked about 1,200 and divided them up among the 17 ships. But while we may call them "ships," in reality they were very small vessels. Even the largest among them was shorter than 100 feet, and many probably measured between 50 and 70 feet. You could have put two of them side by side on a modern basketball court and had a little extra room all the way around.

The ships were built up both in the bow and the stern, which made them slightly top-heavy. As soon as they reached the open sea, they would begin to roll. That was nothing new to the crew, who were all experienced sailors.

But for the passengers, most of whom had never been to sea, the motion was very unsettling. So even before the Spanish coast dropped from view behind them, many of them were seasick. Soon, however, most of them gained their "sea legs," and they could tolerate the constant motion.

A few days later, land loomed on the horizon. But it wasn't the New World. It was the Canary Islands, located off the west coast of Africa. Columbus spent several days loading up last-minute supplies, then departed. On October 13, the final island faded from sight behind the ships. They were alone, following what would become the traditional sailing route from Europe to the New World: "Sail south until the butter melts, then head due west." Navigation instruments were extremely primitive, so the ships' pilots used their years of experience at sea to make educated guesses about their position.

Shipboard life quickly settled into a long-established pattern of men at sea. The crew members were divided into two watches. Each watch would be on duty for four hours, then have four hours to relax. In Columbus' time, the watches changed at 3:00, 7:00, and 11:00. The only exception would have been during the afternoon, when two-hour "dog watches" replaced the usual four-hour periods. That way, the two watches alternated the very unpopular "graveyard watch" from 11:00 P.M. to 3:00 A.M.

How did they tell the time? They used what was called an *ampoletta* or *reloj de arena*, a type of hourglass in which the sand would run from the upper to the lower portion in half an hour. A ship's boy was assigned to turn it over as soon as the sand ran out. Sometimes he would forget to do that, or he would lose count of the number of turns he'd made, causing occasional confusion and problems.

The men knew that their very first duty when they came on watch was to pump the ship, because wooden ships constantly leaked and there was always some water in the bilge. Then they would perform their other duties—make minor repairs, adjust the sails, and do whatever else was necessary to keep the ship running through the water as efficiently as possible. The men who were on watch at dawn had an extra duty: Before calling the next watch, they had to scrub down the deck using seawater they'd haul up in heavy wooden buckets.

The fresh food they had taken aboard at the Canary Islands was quickly eaten. If they were lucky, they might catch a few fish along the way. Otherwise, their food was very bad for nearly the entire voyage. The only way of preserving food at that time was to salt it very heavily. Of course, eating salted food makes a person extra thirsty. But because of the small size of the ships and the number of men who were aboard, the amount of drinking water had to be carefully limited. As a result, everyone was almost constantly thirsty. And they soon became accustomed to an extra "delicacy" in the ship's biscuits, or hardtack, that they ate almost every day: maggots and other kinds of insect larvae.

So it was understandable that they were excited to see land. Besides providing an end to the boredom and cramped conditions aboard the tiny ships, land meant fresh food and fresh water—all the men could eat and drink.

But they had to curb their impatience. After his first landing in October 1492, Columbus had turned southward and spent several weeks cruising through what we now call the Caribbean Sea. He discovered Cuba and then an island he called La Isla Española. Today it is known as Hispaniola, and the nations of Haiti and the Dominican Republic are located there.

While he was exploring these new waters, the *Santa Maria*, his largest ship, was caught on a reef and wrecked. All the men had to crowd onto the two remaining ships. Columbus was afraid that they couldn't all return to Spain. He left about 40 of them behind in a settlement he called La Villa de la Navidad (Nativity Town), which was founded during the Christmas season.

Not surprisingly, Columbus was eager to see those men again. But he quickly realized that his fleet had drifted a little south, and what they were seeing was not Española but a new island. He named it Dominica, the Latin word for "Sunday," after the day of the week on which it was sighted.

Columbus quickly claimed it in the name of King Ferdinand and Queen Isabella of Spain, then headed north.

Soon he discovered a much larger island that lay to the east of Española, modern-day Puerto Rico. (In Spanish, *puerto rico* means "rich port.") Its Indian inhabitants called it Borinquen, and Columbus named it San Juan Bautista, after St. John the Baptist. The fleet stopped briefly to take on fresh water.

Columbus pushed on. Soon the fleet arrived off Navidad, but something was wrong. Even though the ships were in plain sight for a long time, no one rushed down to the beach to welcome them.

Cautiously, some of the best soldiers went ashore. It didn't take them long to find out why no one had come down to meet them. Every one of the Spaniards who had been left behind was dead.

The Indians explained what had happened. The Spaniards hadn't settled down and established farms, which Columbus had wanted them to do. Instead, they became greedy and tried to get their hands on gold. But they didn't want to do the work themselves. They forced the Indians to do the hard work for them. They even stole jewelry from the Indians. And they treated them very harshly.

After a while the Indians had had enough. They banded together and killed the Spaniards. But even though they had killed his men, they still welcomed Columbus. The ships all anchored and the sailors went ashore.

One of these sailors was Juan Ponce de León (wahn ponts day LEE-on or wahn pont-suh DAY lee-OWN).■

A portrait of Juan Ponce de León as a relatively young man, full of confidence. He wears armor typical of the times.

THE YOUNG WARRIOR

J uan Ponce de León may have arrived in the New World while he was still a teenager. Because the birth records from that era are very confusing, it is not definite when he was born. Some people put his date of birth as early as 1460, although it is much more likely that it took place considerably later, probably in 1474. If so, he was only 19 when he took his first steps on Española.

We are not even sure about his parents' names, although the best guess is that his father was Pedro Ponce de León and his mother was Doña Leonor de Figueroa. His birthplace was apparently the village of San Tervas de Campos, about 35 miles west of Palencia in the northwest corner of what is now the province of Valladolid. He was born into an important family: The Ponces could trace their roots back at least 500 years.

He was also born into a world that was at war.

In the year 711, the Moors of North Africa, who practiced the religion of Islam, came across the narrow Strait of

Gibraltar into Christian Spain and conquered it. The Spaniards resented the fact that foreigners ruled their country—
and what was worse, foreigners who believed in another
religion. Almost immediately the Spaniards began the
Reconquista (reconquest), and Spain was in an almost con-
tinuous state of war after that.

Juan Ponce de León was probably well educated, at least
by the standards of the times. But what the times really
demanded were fighting men. Juan was a fit young man
from a well-known family. One of his older relatives was
Rodrigo Ponce de León, who had already become a hero
fighting against the Moors.

It was natural that Juan Ponce would become involved in
the fighting. He served with a knight named Don Pedro
Núñez de Guzmán, and probably began as a page. Pages
were boys of noble birth who were hired to act practically as
servants. They waited on tables, cleaned up dirty clothes,
and did other menial chores. But unlike most other servants,
who would have performed those duties for their entire
lives, Ponce and other pages were servants for only a couple
of years. They were rewarded with a room, meals, and les-
sons in fighting.

Soon Juan Ponce became a squire, or knight's helper.
Squires went into battle with the knights they served, assist-
ing them with their weapons and armor. When they were not
in battle, squires trained with swords, spears, and lances for
the day that they would become knights themselves. Tradi-
tionally, boys became squires by the age of 13 or 14, so
young Ponce would have fought during the final few years
of the war against the Moors.

That war finally ended in early 1492, when the Moors
surrendered Granada, the last piece of Spanish territory they
controlled.

While the Spanish were excited that they had finally reclaimed all their territory, there was one unfortunate side effect. Thousands of knights and other fighting men suddenly found themselves out of work.

A few of them were the eldest sons in their families. That meant that their futures were secure. They would inherit the family properties and estates when their fathers died.

But most of them, such as Juan Ponce de León, were second, third, and even younger sons. They could become priests, but that wasn't a very appealing way of life for men who had been fighting for many years. And the thought of actually working with their hands had no attraction for them.

As a result, Columbus' timing couldn't have been better. When he returned from his first voyage and word began circulating that he was looking for men to accompany him on another expedition, many of these newly unemployed fighters were eager to join him.

Going to the New World to find adventure, to fight, to become rich—now *that* was something they could sink their teeth into. It was no wonder that Columbus had far more volunteers than he could take.

As Robert H. Fuson notes in *Juan Ponce de León and the Spanish Discovery of Puerto Rico and Florida*, one biographer of Ponce wrote, "[Juan Ponce] was a squire without a source of wealth, a veteran of the Conquest of Granada, in search of fame, honor, adventure, and future, like the great majority of Conquistadores whether of good lineage or not."

In short, he was exactly the type of man that Columbus was looking for to accompany him to the New World.■

FREY NICOLAS DE OVANDO

*This statue of Nicolás de Ovando stands in the Plaza de España.
Nicolás de Ovando was sent to Española in 1502 to increase the
amount of wealth sent back to Spain and to make Española safe
for the Spaniards.*

THE GOVERNOR

Because men such as Juan Ponce were experienced in fighting, and also because there were so many more Spaniards than native peoples at Navidad, there wasn't much chance that this expedition would suffer the same fate as the unfortunate few who had been killed there earlier.

Columbus decided against trying to rebuild the ruined town. He turned east again and established another settlement about 40 miles away the week before Christmas. He christened this town Isabela in honor of the Spanish queen. Isabela would soon be followed by other settlements as the Spanish began to spread out over Española.

We know very little about Juan Ponce's early life, but we know nothing of what role—if any—the young man played in the first few years of this increasing Spanish control. It is possible, even likely, that he returned to Spain at some point during this time.

What we do know is that Columbus did not produce enough riches from his new colony to satisfy the king and queen. He had raised expectations so high that what he was able to send back was not sufficient. In addition, some of the colonists sent letters denouncing him back to Spain.

In 1499, Ferdinand and Isabella sent a royal commissioner, Francisco de Bobadilla, to improve the situation.

A portrait of Queen Isabella, after whom Columbus named his new town in Española. She was born in 1451 and married King Ferdinand in 1469. They completed the re-conquest of Spain from the Moors and also provided the funds for Columbus' voyages of discovery. Isabella died in 1504.

Bobadilla didn't do anything to make the colony more profitable, but he did send Columbus back to Spain in chains. Ferdinand and Isabella were very unhappy at this harsh treatment, so they freed Columbus and gave his titles back to him. However, rather than send him back to Española as governor, they selected a man named Nicolás de Ovando to be the new governor.

Ovando sailed for Española early in 1502 with 32 ships and 2,500 men. Many believe that Juan Ponce was part of this expedition, which was nearly destroyed by a vicious storm but managed to survive with the loss of only one ship.

Ovando had two primary missions: to increase the amount of gold and other wealth being sent back to Spain and to make Española "safe" for the Spaniards. The first mission meant using some of the local Indians, a tribe known as the Taino, to do the hard work of mining the gold. The second meant killing the others outright, driving them even farther into the mountains, or sending them back to Spain as slaves.

It also meant that Juan Ponce began to make his mark on history.

In 1504, he led a campaign against the Indians in the province of Higüey at the eastern end of Española. Even though his men were outnumbered, they were skilled, ruthless warriors who were heavily armed with swords, lances, crossbows, and primitive muskets. They had body armor, which protected them from arrows. They had horses, which made them seem bigger than they actually were. They also had large, fierce dogs, which they used to hunt down the Indians.

It didn't take long for Ponce and the other soldiers to overcome the feeble resistance put up by the Indians. Ovando, impressed by what Ponce had accomplished, granted him enough land to establish a plantation. He allowed him to use Indians to work the land. And he named him *adelantado* (governor) of the province.

Unlike most of his fellow Spaniards, Ponce apparently realized that there were other ways of becoming rich in this new world than by seeking gold. He seems to have been wise enough to ask the Indians' advice on the best ways to work the land and fair enough to treat his Indian workers relatively decently. As a result, his plantation prospered. He grew sugar cane, sweet potatoes, and maize, a type of corn. He also raised livestock. He shipped his produce and meat back to Spain. Because his plantation was located near a port, ships stopping for provisions would purchase what they needed from him. He soon became wealthy.

By this time, Ponce was married. His wife, Lenore, had been born in Spain but came to the New World with her father, who opened an inn in Española. Ponce and Lenore would have four children—Juana, Isabel, María, and Luis.

In 1505, Ovando gave Ponce permission to establish the 16th town in Española. He decided on a site near his plantation and named his new settlement Salvaleón, after one of his maternal grandfather's titles in Spain—Lord of Salvaleón. He built a large stone house, which still stands.

He still hoped that one day he might find gold and become even richer. He began casting his eye eastward, toward San Juan Bautista. It lay about 80 miles east of Española, and Ponce remembered his brief visit there in 1493.

In 1506, with Ovando's backing and approval, Ponce led an expedition to San Juan Bautista. The men landed at the same spot where Columbus had halted briefly for water more than a decade earlier. They sent out scouting parties, which found some gold, though not in the abundance they had hoped for. Then the men marched overland to a point near the present-day Puerto Rican capitol of San Juan, where they established a small settlement called Caparra. Soon afterward, Ponce and most of the men returned to Española.

The following year, 1508, Ponce returned, leading another expedition. Though Caparra had been abandoned, the new group reestablished it and resumed the hunt for gold. Ponce brought his family with him, put up a new stone house, and established another plantation.

Soon events beyond Ponce's control began to intervene. Columbus had died in 1506, and three years later his son Don Diego Columbus returned to Española to reclaim his late father's titles. This began a legal struggle with King Ferdinand. Diego technically had authority over San Juan Bautista because it was one of the islands his father had discovered. However, the courts ordered him not to interfere with Ponce, who had been appointed the island's governor by King Ferdinand.

The uneasy situation continued for more than two years. Then, in late 1511, Don Diego won a legal victory—all of his father's titles, rights, and privileges were awarded to him. That meant he would have supreme power in San Juan Bautista. He wasted little time in installing his own man as governor. Ponce remained the island's military captain, and as a favorite of King Ferdinand he enjoyed additional protection.

Still, he wanted to find a way out of what was becoming an increasingly difficult situation. It was hard trying to get along with a man who clearly didn't want him around.

Somewhat ironically, it was Christopher Columbus himself who provided the solution to the dilemma that had arisen between his son and Ponce.■

This woodcut illustrates the search for the Fountain of Youth during Ponce de León's first expedition in 1513. At that time, people still believed that this new land was an island.

THE FOUNTAIN OF YOUTH

During his first voyage of discovery in 1492, Columbus had been heading straight for the North American continent when he changed his course to the southwest. Five days later, he landed at the island of San Salvador.

The very next day, he wrote in his logbook, "The natives here have indicated to me that not only is there land to the south and southwest, but also to the northwest. . . . Furthermore, if I understand correctly, it is from the northwest that strangers come to fight and capture the people here."

However, he decided to head almost directly south when he left San Salvador. He missed his chance to become the first European to stand on future U.S. soil.

Ever since he made that fateful decision, rumors persisted that there was a large, unknown landmass lying northwest of Española. This unknown land—which eventually became known as Bimini—soon acquired a reputation for having vast riches. The Bahama Islands, which include San Salvador and also lie to the northwest, were already relatively well known. For the most part, they were small. And the Indians who lived there were very poor. Bimini, the Spaniards reasoned, must have been even farther northwest.

These rumors had reached King Ferdinand, who—as always—was interested in any scheme that had the possibility of bringing more wealth to Spain. In addition, he seems to have been genuinely appreciative of the loyalty and devoted service that Ponce had always given him.

He was very aware of what was going on between Diego Columbus and Ponce de León. He also knew that Bartholomew Columbus, Christopher's brother and Diego's uncle, wanted to try to locate Bimini. But Ferdinand believed that the Columbus family already had enough land and power. He sent a trusted messenger to ask Ponce if he would be interested in leading an expedition to search for this wondrous island.

Ponce could have simply gone back to his original plantation on Española, but he and his family had moved to San Juan Bautista. Perhaps he believed that finding Bimini would increase the strength of his position with respect to Diego Columbus. And as a man of action ever since his early teens, the thought of new adventures in uncharted waters must have been exciting to him. He agreed to lead the expedition.

King Ferdinand sent Ponce a contract in early 1512 that spelled out his rights and obligations. Ponce had the exclusive right for three years to try to discover Bimini. He would be the governor of any new lands he might discover. He would be entitled to a share of the profits resulting from his discovery. And he had to pay the entire cost of fitting out the expedition.

There were rumors of another type of wealth on Bimini. According to these rumors, there was a fountain, a natural spring in the ground. If someone swam in it or drank the water from it, that person would regain his or her youth.

Ponce was probably suspicious of this rumor. He couldn't find anyone who had actually drunk from this spring. If it really existed, why weren't the islands full of people who were several centuries old?

It is possible that the Indians invented the story in an effort to get rid of the Spaniards. They already believed that the Spaniards were a little crazy because of their love for gold. To the Indians, gold was just pretty yellow pebbles. But the Spanish wanted gold so much that they were making the Indians' lives miserable. Perhaps the Indians hoped that if they could convince the Spaniards of the existence of this "fountain of youth" on Bimini, in addition to the gold that was supposedly there, they would sail away and leave them alone.

There is another possibility. When the Spanish arrived, they inadvertently brought diseases such as smallpox with them. The Indians were helpless against these germs. For every Indian killed in a direct battle, more perished through disease. The Spanish had built up immunity to those diseases and were not affected. The Indians may have believed that Catholic "magic" was stronger than their own, because those who believed in it didn't get sick and die. Because the Catholics practiced baptism, the Indians may have believed that the water they used had special curative powers. Perhaps they thought that similar waters existed in their own lands and all they had to do was find them.

A third possibility is that the Spaniards simply misunderstood what the Indians were saying, or the other way around. If a Spaniard asked an Indian about a "miraculous" fountain of youth, the Indian, not understanding what *miraculous* really meant, might have assumed that the Spaniard was simply asking where he could get a drink of water.

We don't know if Ponce actually believed in the Fountain of Youth. But as he had already demonstrated, he was a successful planter who had become rich by shipping his products back to Spain. If he could find this supposed fountain, he would become wealthy far beyond his wildest dreams by adding the water to the rest of his shipments.

Whether or not Ponce believed that the Fountain of Youth existed, the fountain certainly was not his main reason for seeking Bimini. In the contract Ferdinand sent him, there isn't a single mention of *El Fuente*, as the Fountain of Youth was commonly known.

Even though the fountain was not an official part of the contract, King Ferdinand almost certainly hoped that Ponce would find it. Queen Isabella had died in 1504, and soon afterward the king—by then in his mid-50s—had married a woman 35 years younger than he.

And Ponce himself may have started to feel the effects of aging. Even if he had been born as late as 1474, he would by then have been nearly 40. Perhaps he was starting to develop a few gray hairs himself.

The expedition cost a great deal of money. Because he had to pay the entire cost, Ponce needed to be fairly confident that he could make his money back. Crops and gold were two things in which he had much experience. As a successful planter, he knew that if he could establish similar plantations in Bimini, he could make money. If he found gold, that would add to his potential profit.

But the fountain wasn't something he could feel as confident about. He probably thought, "If I can find it, fine. But if not, I won't be too disappointed."

He was much more concerned with putting together his fleet of three ships—*Santa Maria de Consolación, Santiago,* and *San Cristóbal*—and making sure that he had enough men to go with him. He also had to provide plenty of provisions for several months of explorations. And there was something else to consider: Although he was in charge of the expedition, just as Columbus had been in command during his four voyages, there was one difference between the two men. Columbus was an experienced seaman and navigator. Ponce wasn't. He hired Antonio Alaminos to be his pilot.

By the end of 1512, Ponce was spending most of his time on last-minute preparations. He traveled back to Española to ensure that his plantation at Salvaleón could provide enough food. He kept recruiting men and making sure that they were properly outfitted and carried enough weapons. He supervised the final loading of his ships and conferred with their captains to guarantee that they would stand up to the dangers of venturing into uncharted oceans. And in his few spare moments, he probably dreamed a little. . . .

Even if there was no Fountain of Youth, there was little doubt that there were more islands to conquer. Maybe he would find gold. Almost certainly he would find more fertile lands, and this time he wouldn't have to contend with the son of Christopher Columbus to keep them. If he could discover Bimini, he would finally become top dog.■

This famous painting by Thomas Moran shows Ponce de León in Florida. But most of the time, the Native Americans he met didn't sit peacefully at his feet. He had to be constantly on watch.

THE FEAST OF FLOWERS

The little fleet departed from San Juan Bautista on March 3, 1513, heading in a northwesterly direction. Within a few days the sailors began seeing islands, most of which would have appeared on Alaminos' charts. The Bahamas are filled with shoals and reefs, making navigation at night dangerous. The ships probably anchored every evening, giving the men the opportunity to go ashore.

About two weeks after their departure, they reached the island of San Salvador, where Columbus had first landed 21 years earlier. They stayed at San Salvador for a week or even longer, taking on additional water. Then they set sail into the unknown. On March 27, they saw a small island that they couldn't identify off in the distance. Because it was far too small to be Bimini, they paid little regard to it and continued on their way. Then they were in the open sea. They were the first Europeans to pass this way, and nobody knew what lay ahead.

Six days later, on April 2, 1513, the cry of *"Tierra! Tierra!"* rang out from a lookout. The low coastline lying dead ahead stretched along the horizon in both directions as far as the eye could see. Soon the three ships were sailing just off-shore. They looked for a harbor but couldn't find any, so they finally anchored for the night.

Early the next morning, Ponce and most of the men rowed ashore in small boats. The beach was long and sandy. Behind it were thick green trees and flowers in full bloom. But there were no Indians. Ponce claimed the land for Spain and put up a banner.

As head of the expedition, Ponce had to decide what to call this new land. According to the ship's log, "believing that this land was an island, they named it La Florida, be-cause it was very pretty to behold with many refreshing trees, and it was flat, and unvarying, and because moreover, they discovered it in the time of the Feast of Flowers [*Pascua Florida*, which is Easter]."

Even though this land was exactly where Bimini was supposed to be, Ponce did not confer that name on it. More likely, he regarded it as another island—and as his later explorations would indicate, a very large island.

Where did they land? It was probably somewhere be-tween modern-day Daytona Beach and Melbourne Beach, not too far from Cape Canaveral.

Believing that he had discovered an island, Ponce spent several days at his original anchorage, then began sailing slowly south along the coast. He found very little to interest him. There were no harbors and still no Indians. Nearly three weeks after his first landfall, he approached what he called Cabo de los Corrientes (Cape of the Currents). The northward-flowing current was so strong that his ships couldn't make any headway even with the wind behind them. Two ships were close enough to shore to be able to anchor. But the third—the *San Cristóbal*—was carried out of sight to the north. This marked the discovery of the Gulf Stream, a powerful current that flows for hundreds of miles between the Caribbean and the North Atlantic.

It also marked Ponce's first contact with the local Indians while he was waiting for the *San Cristóbal* to return.

"Juan Ponce went ashore here," the logbook records, "and was called by the Indians who, in turn, tried to take the small boat, the oars, and arms. Because he did not want to start a fight, he had to tolerate their taunts. And, he wanted to establish a good first impression. But because the Indians hit a sailor in the head with a stick, knocking him unconscious, he [Juan Ponce] had to fight with them. The Indians, with their arrows and spears, wounded two Castilians [Spaniards], and the Indians received little damage."

This wasn't an isolated incident. A day or two later, while a work party was ashore collecting firewood and water, a party of 60 Native Americans attacked. The outcome was a little more favorable this time, as Ponce was able to capture one of the attackers to act as a guide.

Soon the *San Cristóbal* was able to claw her way back down the coast and rejoin the others. Two and a half weeks after their first encounter with the Gulf Stream, the three ships finally had enough wind to get around Cabo de los Corrientes. As they sailed south, they eventually reached the area that is now Miami. Still following the coastline, they sailed along the Florida Keys. To Ponce, the small islands seemed to resemble men who were suffering and twisted in pain, so he called them *Los Mártires* (The Martyrs), after his countrymen who had perished in the war against the Moors. This name proved to be prophetic, because later explorers who survived shipwrecks and struggled ashore in this area were almost always killed by Indians.

When Ponce passed what is now Key West, he turned northward and began exploring the west coast of Florida. By then it seemed obvious that he had discovered a very large island indeed.

He spent about three weeks in the area of Sanibel Island and San Carlos Bay, about 120 miles almost directly north of Key West. Alaminos carefully charted the bay, and it became an important destination for future Spanish explorers.

During this time, Ponce had several contacts with the very warlike Calusa Indians and their chieftain, who became known as Carlos. Learning that Carlos had gold that he claimed to want to trade with the Spanish, Ponce nearly fell into a trap. The Indians attacked with more than 20 canoes filled with warriors. Some tried to pin down the men on deck while others tried to cut the anchor lines and drag the ships away. But this attack, and another one a few days later, was driven off.

By then, Ponce seemed to realize he wasn't going to make much headway in exploring this new land. He didn't have enough men to explore inland because of the constant threat of Indian attack, so he didn't know if there was gold to be found. And he certainly hadn't come close to even beginning a search for the Fountain of Youth.

In addition, his ships were starting to leak. The only way to repair them was to deliberately run them aground, fasten ropes to the sides, and pull them over onto their sides. It was hard work and required a lot of men. That wouldn't leave very many to guard against attacks from the Indians.

Ponce decided to continue his search for Bimini, but away from this dangerous place. He headed south and stopped briefly at what he called the Tortugas, as that was the Spanish name for the large loggerhead turtles he found in abundance there. The men killed nearly 200 tortugas to provide fresh meat.

He sailed east along the coastline of Cuba, then returned to the Bahamas for several more weeks of exploration. Finally he headed back for San Juan Bautista. Meanwhile he sent the *San Cristóbal*—the smallest, most maneuverable of the three ships—by herself in a futile, final effort to locate Bimini and *El Fuente* (the fountain).

He was in for a rude surprise when he returned. His house had been burned to the ground and his family had nearly been destroyed.■

This illustration portrays King Ferdinand and Queen Isabella. King Ferdinand and Germaine de Foix, whom Ferdinand married after Isabella's death, made Ponce de León a knight. They also named him governor of both Florida and Bimini. Then they presented him with a coat of arms. He was the first conquistador to receive such an honor.

CHAPTER 6

THE RETURN TO FLORIDA

While Ponce was away, the settlement of Caparra had been attacked and destroyed by a party of Carib Indians from another island. Diego Columbus, his old enemy, had seized on this incident to try to discredit Ponce even more. He accused Ponce of raising the settlement in a place that was hard to defend. Diego also wanted to expand his own power.

Ponce realized that he would have a hard time defending himself when he was surrounded by enemies. He sailed back to Spain in the spring of 1514 to give King Ferdinand a firsthand report of what he had found during his voyage and to give his side of the story of the attack. He wanted to go over his contract with the king to make sure that he still had the power to colonize the new land. He also wanted to be sure he retained his rights and titles in Española and San Juan Bautista in spite of the nasty things that Diego Columbus was saying about him.

Ferdinand greeted him warmly. He made him a knight and presented him with a coat of arms, the first conquistador to receive those honors. He was now Don Juan Ponce de León.

Ponce and Ferdinand also signed several documents. Don Ponce was appointed as the governor of both Florida and Bimini, since by that time he had concluded that the two islands were different.

Part of the new contract stated that Ponce was "to bring them [the Indians] to understand our Catholic Faith, and to obey and serve it as they are obliged to."

That meant that every time Ponce encountered a new group of Natives, he had to read a several-hundred-word document called *El Requerimiento* (The Requirement). This document informed the Indians that they were now subjects of the king and queen of Spain. It also summarized the beliefs of the Catholic Church and required the Indians "of their own free will" to become members of the church. If they resisted either of these conditions, the Spaniards were justified in making war against them—and in selling them into slavery.

Ponce may have shuddered at the thought of standing in front of the belligerent Calusa Indians and spending ten minutes reading this document to them. His previous encounters suggested that the Indians had no interest in becoming either Spanish subjects or members of the Catholic Church. And he would need many more men than had accompanied him the first time to wage a successful war against them.

In addition, there was a very heavy string attached to the new contract. Before Ponce could return to Florida, the king said, he had to lead an army against the Caribs. The Caribs, who had a reputation for being cannibals, were far fiercer than the Taino and had terrorized a number of outlying Spanish settlements. They had also nearly killed Ponce's own family. A military campaign to put down the Caribs seemed to be the answer. Ponce departed from Spain in 1515 to assume those duties.

Not long after Ponce began his campaign, King Ferdinand died. Ponce wasn't sure if his agreement to develop Florida still stood. He had to go back to Spain at the end of 1516 to meet with the new king, Charles I. He spent well over a year there before he was satisfied, not returning until the middle of 1518.

By the time he returned to San Juan Bautista, he had to spend a great deal of time on his plantation. There were the usual political squabbles that demanded his time and energy. And it took yet more time to outfit the new expedition. He had to arrange for ships, recruit men, and purchase all the supplies they would require to carve out a new settlement. They needed everything from plows and seeds and livestock to weapons.

By then, Ponce must have felt that time was starting to run out. In the years since he had returned from his voyage of discovery to Florida, other explorers had ventured into the same region. They had settled Cuba, which lay just 90 miles from Florida. Some men had pushed into the Gulf of Mexico. More and more, they began to believe that Florida wasn't an island but a large peninsula that was part of a much larger continent. It was becoming increasingly obvious to Ponce that he would have to make a move soon to establish a colony or risk losing it to other conquistadores.

There was yet another reason he couldn't leave earlier. His wife had died, probably in 1519. As he explained in a letter to Adrian, then the bishop of Tortosa (in 1522 he would become Pope Adrian VI), "The difficulties that have befallen me are thereby [related to] having become a widower and left with daughters that I did not wish to leave nor abandon until they were married. And now they are married, may it please God."

Finally, in early 1521, all was in readiness. Ponce had two ships, which he packed as full as he could with at least 100 men, supplies, and horses, cattle, sheep, pigs, and goats. The tiny vessels, probably less than 80 feet long and no more than 25 feet wide, must have been very crowded.

Juan Ponce de León and his men being attacked by Indians in Florida. The Spaniards were normally better armed than the Indians. So the Indians would often set ambushes and fire their arrows from concealed positions.

Unlike his earlier voyage, which was well documented, very little is known about what happened on this second trip. We know when it began and approximately when it ended, but nearly everything that happened in between is shrouded in mystery. There is also a suggestion that it not only cost more than the first voyage, but also put a severe strain on Ponce's resources. Perhaps being gone from his plantations for so long meant that they produced fewer crops and less livestock.

A large band of Indians attacked Ponce and his colonists soon after they landed in 1521. Ponce himself was seriously wounded in the leg by an arrow. It may have been poisoned. His men carried him back to the ship to return to Cuba.

This photograph shows the interior of the San Juan Cathedral in San Juan, Puerto Rico. The remains of Juan Ponce de León are there today.

The two ships departed from what is now San Juan on February 20, 1521. Ponce decided that they would sail up the west coast of Florida and establish a colony. Probably they landed sometime in mid-March, but there are virtually no clues as to what spot along more than 300 miles of coastline was the site of the little settlement.

Probably the Spaniards spent much of their time ashore either fighting off Indians or worrying about when the next attack might come. And finally, in what was probably late June or early July, the little band of colonists was overwhelmed. Some were killed, others wounded. The most serious wound happened to Ponce himself. He was struck in the upper thigh with an arrow. The wound was painful and he couldn't stand up. His men carried him back to the beach, then rowed him out to one of the two ships. Without their leader, the Spanish felt defenseless. They abandoned the colony, salvaged what they could, and sailed away.

Ponce's injury did not heal. Perhaps the arrow had been poisoned. By the time the two ships arrived in Havana, Cuba, the closest Spanish settlement, the infection had become too severe to be dealt with by the primitive medicine of that time. Ponce died soon afterward, probably about mid-July 1521, and was buried in Havana. Nearly 40 years later, his remains were exhumed and carried back to the Cathedral of San José in Puerto Rico, where they remained for more than three centuries. In 1908, his body was reburied in a marble tomb in the larger Cathedral of San Juan.■

Panfilo de Narváez led an expedition to Florida in 1526. He signed a contract to establish settlements for Spain between Florida and Mexico. But it was poorly organized and de Narváez made some very bad decisions after his arrival. Of his 600 men, all but four died.

THE LEGACY OF JUAN PONCE DE LEON

Most people think of Juan Ponce de León in connection with the Fountain of Youth. They believe that he spent years in Florida, hacking back and forth through the wilderness trying to find something that never did exist. But that belief is obviously not correct. In two separate voyages, he spent a total of less than one year in Florida. For much of that time he was aboard his ships, voyaging from one anchorage to another. When he did go ashore, he was primarily concerned with keeping watch for hostile Indians.

There are paintings of his supposed search. They show small groups of well-dressed men at different springs and streams, drinking samples of the water at each location. The scene is tranquil and peaceful, as if the men have nothing

Many drawings such as this exist, portraying Juan Ponce de León searching for the Fountain of Youth. A natural fresh water pool just south of Daytona Beach that he may have discovered is known today as Ponce de Leon Springs. It is open for swimming, boating and fishing.

else to do besides sip water. The reality, of course, was considerably different. Ponce's men probably were a pretty scruffy-looking bunch, living in the same clothes for weeks on end. And rather than trying to find something that would turn back the clock and make them younger, they were probably more concerned with just hanging on to the lives they had at the present moment.

While there is no such thing as the Fountain of Youth, Florida has dozens of natural springs where virtually transparent water continually bubbles to the surface. During the centuries before the arrival of Columbus, there was probably some traffic back and forth between the Bahamas and Florida. Word of those fountainlike springs—natural forerunners of modern hot tubs, which must have been very pleasant places to relax and soothe sore muscles—may have made its way back to the islands. With a little embellishment, their curative powers could have evolved in the legend that the Indians passed on to the Spaniards.

Although Ponce did not find the Fountain of Youth, he did discover something else that involved water: the Gulf Stream. While he didn't fully realize its significance—more than anything else it was a nuisance that delayed his exploration for a few weeks—his pilot Alaminos used it six years later to pioneer a much faster way for the treasure-laden Spanish galleons to get home.

Hernán Cortés, who had just begun what would eventually be the conquest of Mexico, was eager to get his first load of treasure back to Spain. Alaminos, who was working as Cortés' pilot, took a gamble. Remembering the swift current he'd encountered off the Florida coast, he took the ship in that direction. To his surprise and delight, the current extended well beyond Florida, eventually curving to the east, and helped carry his ship back to Spain faster than any previous ship. That same route was adopted on almost every future voyage. In a sense, we can say that Columbus pioneered the way from Spain to the New World, and Ponce de León discovered the best way to get back.

Ponce's discovery of Florida also indirectly paved the way for another great Spanish exploration. It began in 1526 when Panfilo de Narváez signed a contract from Charles I to establish settlements between Florida and Mexico—a huge sweep of well over 1,000 miles along the shoreline of the Gulf of Mexico. Narváez began with more than 400 men, but dogged by bad decisions and even worse luck, all but four died in 1528. Those four survivors lived with a number of Indian tribes for eight years before they were discovered in western Mexico. During their travels, they heard reports of the supposed great riches of the Seven Cities of Cibola, though they hadn't actually seen them in person. But those secondhand stories were directly responsible for Francisco Vásquez de Coronado's two-year expedition that began in Mexico in 1540 and went through present-day Arizona and New Mexico as far as Kansas.

This statue of Juan Ponce de León stands in Old San Juan, Puerto Rico. Ponce de León led the first Spanish expedition to the island. The city of Ponce, near the island's southern coast, was founded by his great-grandson and today is the island's second-largest city, with a population of nearly 200,000.

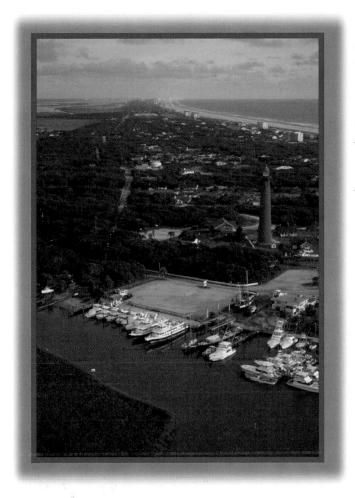

Ponce Inlet in Daytona Beach, Florida. It is located near the spot where many historians believe that Ponce de León came ashore for the first time in 1513. It is one of several sites in Florida that are named for Ponce de León.

Like Ponce, Coronado was generally regarded as a failure. Yet today, both men are among the most famous 16th-century Spanish explorers.

While most of the names that Ponce bestowed on the places he discovered in Florida have long since been changed, his name for the state itself has remained for nearly 500 years. In addition, several place names honor him. Even though he never set foot there, Leon County in northern Florida—where the state capital of Tallahassee is located—honors the state's discoverer. Perhaps he dropped anchor in Ponce de León Bay on Florida's southwest coast. The city of

This is the most famous portrait of Juan Ponce de León. It is taken from a woodcut in a book that was published in 1728.

Ponce, on Puerto Rico's southern coast, was founded in 1692 by Ponce's great-grandson. And there are others.

Ponce failed to establish a colony in Florida, because he was consistently foiled by the Calusa Indians. These people resisted all European efforts to intrude into their territory for more than 200 years after Ponce appeared.

While many, if not most, Spaniards who voyaged to the New World in the first few years after Columbus' arrival came in search of relatively easy money, Juan Ponce de León appears to have been a somewhat exceptional man. He did become wealthy, but not by discovering gold. He worked the land. Though he could be harsh and cruel when he was fighting the local Indians, he seems to have treated them decently when they worked on his plantations.

A simple Latin inscription rests next to his burial site in the cathedral of San Juan:

Mole sub hoc fortis
Requiescunt ossa Leónis
Qui vivt factis
Nomina magna suis

Under this sepulcher
Rest the bones of a Lion
Who performed deeds
Even greater than his name ■

CHRONOLOGY

1460–1474	Birth of Juan Ponce de León
1493	Accompanies Christopher Columbus on second voyage to the New World
1504	Leads expedition against Taino Indians and receives land grant
1506	Explores island of San Juan Bautista (now known as Puerto Rico)
1509	Named governor of San Juan Bautista
1511	Replaced as governor of San Juan Bautista
1512	Receives contract to search for Bimini
1513	Discovers Florida
1514	Sails to Spain to meet with King Ferdinand
1515	Returns to New World to lead fight against Carib Indians
1516	Sails to Spain to meet with new king, Charles I
1518	Returns to New World
1521	Leads second expedition to Florida; dies in July from infection following wound from an Indian arrow

TIMELINE IN HISTORY

1492   Moors are driven from Granada, their final foothold in Spain; Christopher Columbus discovers the New World

1493   Columbus begins second expedition

1497   John Cabot, Italian sailor working for England, discovers New foundland

1498   Columbus begins third expedition

1502   Rodrigo de Bastidas explores Caribbean and northern coast of South America; Columbus begins fourth expedition

1506   Columbus dies

1508   Sebastian Cabot, son of John Cabot, explores North American coast; Vicente Yáñez Pinzón and Juan Díaz de Solís sail along the coast of Yucatán

1513   Juan Ponce de León explores Florida Peninsula; Vasco Nuñez de Balboa crosses Isthmus of Panama and becomes first European to view Pacific Ocean

1516   Juan Díaz de Solís locates mouth of Rio de la Plata in South America

1518   Juan de Grijalba sails along eastern coast of Mexico

1519   Ferdinand Magellan begins round-the-world voyage; Hernán Cortés lands in Mexico; Alonzo Alvarez de Pineda explores the Gulf Coast from Florida to Mexico.

1521   Cortés completes conquest of Mexico; Magellan is killed in the Philippine Islands

1522   Magellan's surviving crew members complete voyage around the world

1524   Giovanni da Verrazano explores Atlantic coast from North Carolina to Maine on behalf of France

1540   Francisco Vásquez de Coronado begins exploration of American Southwest in search for legendary Seven Cities of Cibola and eventually reaches Kansas

1542   Juan Rodriguez Cabrillo and Bartolomé Ferrelo explore west coast of North America as far north as Oregon

1551   Real y Pontificia Universidad de Mexico becomes first university on the North American continent

1565   Pedro Menéndez de Avilés establishes St. Augustine, Florida, which becomes oldest U.S. city

FOR FURTHER READING

Crisfield, Deborah. *The Travels of Juan Ponce de León*. Austin, Tex.: Raintree Steck-Vaughn Publishers, 2001.

Dolan, Sean. *Juan Ponce de León*. Philadelphia: Chelsea House Publishers, 1995.

Fuson, Robert H. *Juan Ponce de León and the Spanish Discovery of the New World and Florida*. Blacksburg, Va.: McDonald and Woodward Publishing Company, 2000.

Harmon, Dan. *Juan Ponce de León and the Search for the Fountain of Youth*. Philadelphia: Chelsea House Publishers, 2000.

Heinrichs, Ann. *Ponce de León: Juan Ponce de León Searches for the Fountain of Youth*. Mankato, Minn.: Compass Point Books, 2002.

Manning, Ruth. *Juan Ponce de León*. Chicago: Heinemann Library, 2001.

Morison, Samuel Eliot. *The Great Explorers: The European Discovery of America*. New York: Oxford University Press, 1986.

Peck, Douglas T. *Ponce de León and the Discovery of Florida: The Man, The Myth, and The Truth*. St. Paul, Minn.: Pogo Press, 1993.

Sakurai, Gail. *Juan Ponce de León*. New York: Franklin Watts, Inc., 2001.

ON THE WEB

PBS—Conquistadors
    http://www.pbs.org/opb/conquistadors/

Hispanic Colonization of North America
    http://www.rose-hulman.edu/~delacova/colonization.htm

Hispanic Timeline
    www.getnet.com/~1stbooks/chron3.htm

GLOSSARY

adelantado: the Spanish title for a governor, usually given to someone authorized to explore, settle and rule a territory

belligerent (beh-LIJ-eh-rent): warlike; ready to fight

bilge: the lowest inside part of the hull of a ship

coat of arms: a display honoring an individual or family that contains symbols such as helmets or powerful animals

conquistador (kon-KEES-teh-door): Spanish soldier, usually of noble birth, who was important in conquering Mexico and South America in the late 15th and 16th centuries

crossbow (CROSS-boe): bow fixed crosswise on a wooden stock, which fires short arrows with tremendous force crow's-nest: platform with a protective railing mounted high on the mast of a ship, enabling lookouts to see much farther than they could on deck

exhume (ex-OOM): to dig something out of the earth that was buried

hardtack: a kind of biscuit or bread made only of flour and water

immunity (ih-MEW-nuh-tee): not being affected by a disease

martyr (MAR-tur): a person who endures suffering and death for a cause he or she believes in

menial (MEE-nee-al): unimportant, low-status, commonplace

plantation (plan-TAY-shun): large estate or farm that produces one or more crops

ruthless (ROOTH-less): showing no mercy or pity

shoals: areas of very shallow water

watch: a period of time for which a specific part of a ship's crew is on duty

INDEX